REST ASSURED

A PRAGMATIC APPROACH TO API DESIGN

Copyright © 2014 By Adam Tuttle

All rights reserved. No part of this book may be reproduced or used in any manner without written permission of the copyright owner except for the use of quotations in a book review. For more information, address: adam@adamtuttle.codes

First paperback edition May 2021.

ISBN 978-1-6780-7641-2

Imprint: Lulu.com

Published by Adam Tuttle

https://restassuredbook.com

REST ASSURED

A PRAGMATIC APPROACH TO API DESIGN

ADAM TUTTLE © 2014

Thank you for supporting an indie author

Thanks for buying my book! If you enjoy it, please post about it on social media. As a self-publishing independent author, I rely heavily on your word of mouth referrals to keep this adventure going.

The book's website is: http://www.restassuredbook.com

If you post that link and some thoughts on what you like about the book, you'll have my unending gratitude. If you tag me in your post (@AdamTuttle on Twitter, adam.tuttle on Facebook), I can even reply to *tell* you how much I appreciate it.

Regardless, I *already* appreciate you buying the book. You rock!

Forward for the second edition

I made many mistakes when I wrote the first edition of REST Assured. Fortunately I had readers like you to point out the typos and grammar mistakes that slipped past my copy editor, Dan. But the bigger mistake was that I believed I had to write something substantial, which is to say lengthy, to make it worth your money.

That's why the first edition included two chapters near the front of the book that are now included only as appendices. Only after many revisions of the book and its website, where I allowed myself to focus on what its value actually is, did I realize that brevity could be a selling point.

For that reason, this second edition is much shorter, more direct, and to the point. I hope you enjoy it.

REST ASSURED
A PRAGMATIC APPROACH TO API DESIGN

Introduction

> "The story so far: In the beginning the Universe was created. This has made a lot of people very angry and been widely regarded as a bad move."
> —Douglas Adams, **The Restaurant at the End of the Universe**

Much has been written on the internet about REST APIs over the years, and much has been written in response with *just enough* italics to give one the impression that the response was written with the bitter taste of anger on the tongue. One thing is for certain: We just can't agree on what qualifies as REST and what does not.

I don't hope to settle these arguments with this book. I do hope to help you make a series of informed pragmatic decisions about how best to get your work done.

I once described XML-RPC to a friend at a work happy-hour and called it REST. Thankfully a more-senior developer stepped in to correct me. A year later, I volunteered to present about REST APIs at a small conference, as a way to motivate myself to learn everything I could about them. Another year later I released a new open source REST API authoring framework for the ColdFusion and Lucee (then "Railo") platforms called Taffy.[1] To this day Taffy remains the most popular choice for authoring REST APIs with CFML.[2] I have since been speaking at user groups and conferences about REST and Taffy, and I continue to act as the lead developer on the project. Still, my research in preparation for this book taught me a few new things.

I told you that story not to stroke my own ego, but to illustrate that we are all in a constant state of learning. We could all do well to remember that someone's choice in design principles *need not* offend us to the point of fervent anger. We can still be friends, even if we

---

[1] http://taffy.io

[2] Using a probably arbitrary, likely subjective, but still the only approximation of a comparison I could come up with: buzz on Twitter and GitHub Contributions and Stars.

disagree on what is REST and what is not; and a friendly attitude might do more to win the support of the masses than any amount of italics could.

In addition to the internet, several books have been written covering REST, but to date I have yet to find one that avoids burying the reader in complex language, academic principles that often don't bear their own weight, and far more words than are necessary to make the point. I hope that I have done better than they.

1: What Is REST, Anyway?

REST, or **RE**presentational **S**tate **T**ransfer, is a method for computer programs to talk to each other over networks. It is a set of generalized conventions that make it easier for API-client developers to understand how to manage data over network protocols —like HTTP— with very little additional context and documentation.

Most developers instantly think about transferring data between web servers and mobile devices, but it was not created for smartphones or even web APIs in general. There is no reason that separate servers can't use REST APIs to shuttle data between themselves, and in fact it is an acceptable, reasonable, and common thing for them to do. REST is a general purpose solution for data management over network connections, so it is ideally suited not only for sharing data between servers and browsers, or servers and mobile devices, but also between servers and other servers.

However, for simplicity's sake and unless otherwise noted, conceptual examples in this book will assume that the client is a web browser. There are some slight deviations when the client is not a web browser, and I will try to point them out whenever possible.

While REST technically should be possible over nearly any protocol, I have never heard of anyone building a REST API over FTP or SSH. Even if you did, it would probably look a lot like tunneling HTTP over FTP, because HTTP and REST have, in practical application and over time, become co-dependent. For the purposes of this book I will simply assume you are using HTTP.

Broadly, there are two phases in REST: the request, and the response. The internet you remember from the early 2000's was a subset of REST. You clicked a link or submitted a form, this request was sent to the server, and the server returned a response. Yes, the HTML `<form>` tag (in combination with your web browser) is a REST client. Today's internet is more complex, and REST continues to grow in popularity, but the traditional "postback" methodology has fallen out of favor as AJAX and Websockets gain in popularity.

Let's establish a vocabulary to make it easier to continue discussing REST concepts with some implied context. A REST request contains up to five things: A noun, a verb (or "method"), a mime type, headers, and data. A response contains a status code, status text, headers, and often some data.

Requests

Nouns

The noun is more commonly referred to as the resource. It identifies the data record(s) that you want to Create, Read, Update, or Delete ("CRUD"). `/widgets` is a noun that identifies the widgets collection, and `/widgets/42` is a noun that identifies a single member of the widgets collection. In both cases, the noun remains constant regardless of the action you are taking upon it, and the verb describes what is being done to it.

Verbs

The verb is what you want to do to your identified resource. The CRUD actions map to specific HTTP verbs: `POST` is for creating new members in a collection, especially if you are *not* specifying the id value of the newly created member. `PUT` is for updating an existing member, or inserting a new member *when you are specifying the id value*. The other two should be pretty self explanatory: `GET` is for reading a resource's data, and `DELETE` is for, yes, deleting it. There are more verbs, but we'll come back to that in a moment.

Each verb is considered either safe, idempotent, or unsafe. Safe requests can be made without fear of altering data or otherwise harming the state of the server. `GET` is safe, because it only reads data and does not change anything. Idempotent verbs are slightly less safe: They change data, but if you repeat the request identically, no additional changes will be made. If you `DELETE` a record, it's gone. If you request to `DELETE` the same record again, no additional data will be deleted. Thus, `DELETE` is idempotent. `PUT` is likewise idempotent. Unsafe verbs make changes every time they are requested. POST-ing a new widget entry will create a new widget with the specified properties each time the request is sent. If you make 3 identical widget POST requests, 3 widget records will be created, even if their attributes are all identical.

Web crawling spiders, like Googlebot, are supposed to be aware of these rules and obey them: They should never submit a form that uses `method="POST"` (because it is unsafe), but can and often do submit forms that use `method="GET"`.

Strictly speaking, you *should* be allowed to use additional verbs in your HTML forms; but earlier browsers either neglected or chose not to implement PUT and DELETE. They are more commonly supported now, however. As we will see soon, AJAX requests commonly make use of additional verbs without issue.

There are a few more less-commonly available standard verbs for REST, and their expected behavior is defined: HEAD is a clone of GET, except that the response data is omitted and only the headers are returned; giving the client the opportunity to decide whether or not they want all of the data. This can be useful with large datasets and well-defined caching mechanisms; something we will explore in another chapter. OPTIONS is a special verb that is used to identify what verbs and headers are allowed for a given resource, in the event that there are restrictions. We will learn more about OPTIONS and how it helps maintain a secure internet in the security chapter. PATCH is the final standard REST verb, and is used to perform an à la carte update: Only the properties provided in the request should be updated, while any properties missing should remain untouched by the request.

If a resource has fifty properties and you make a PUT request against it, you need to include all fifty properties in whatever state you want them to have after the request, even if only changing one of them. Alternatively, you can make a PATCH request and include only the properties you want to change. Aside from the number of

5

properties in the request, and the verb used, they are identical in form and function.

Mime Type

The Mime Type is the way that the client and the API agree on a language in which they will communicate. Back in olden times — when the world was in black and white and all of our parents walked to school barefoot in the snow — XML was popular because it is reasonably easy for computers to parse, and easier for humans to read than fixed-width flat text files.

These days JSON is the golden child, because it is equally human readable (arguably more-so), even easier for many computer languages to parse (almost any ECMAScript[3] variant can simply evaluate the string and get back a native data structure; though this is not considered safe), and most importantly: *faster to transmit*. JSON, or JavaScript Object Notation [4], uses only a few characters to identify different data types where XML used written language. This reduced payload size makes requests and responses faster because less data is transmitted, thereby improving the user experience.[5]

The API supports a fixed and finite set of data formats, and the client may request any one of them to be used. If the client's requested format can not be satisfied, the API default may be used, or an exception may be returned. The client specifies its preferred format in a request header named `Accept`. In order to have the best chance of successful "content negotiation" (picking the format that works best for both the client and the server), clients may provide a prioritized, comma-delimited list with weighted preferences[6] for

---

[3]http://en.wikipedia.org/wiki/ECMAScript

[4]http://json.org/

[5]JSON support is not a requirement for a REST API, nor does it make an API RESTful. API data formats should be viewed as interchangeable. JSON just happens to be popular at the moment because it solves many current problems well.

[6]Including a weight is stupid if you ask me because an ordered list, by

acceptable formats. Each item in the list can be optionally further split into a semicolon-delimited list, with the first sub-item being the requested format and the second representing the weight of the preference.

I just opened my Google Chrome browser and requested google.com. Inspecting the request, I can see that the following `Accept` header was sent:

```
Accept: text/html,
        application/xhtml+xml,
        application/xml;q=0.9,
        image/webp,
        */*;q=0.8
```

This value indicates that equal preference is given to `text/html` and `application/xhtml+xml`. If neither of those is available, then the browser would prefer `application/xml`. If that still isn't availble, for some odd reason, it has requested a WebP image. Don't ask me why, I haven't the foggiest of ideas. Last but not least, it will take whatever you can give it: `*/*`.

Not all response formats are text-based. Binary formats are equally acceptable. You might request a profile in PDF form, or an athlete's highlight reel in video form. You are limited only by your imagination, here.

Headers

Headers are metadata attached to the request and response without being part of the data. They typically represent metadata about the server, the transmission, the data, or the client, but need to remain separate from the body data to avoid confusion and potential

---

definition, indicates some sense of priority. Were I king of the internet, my first decree would be to simplify the `Accept` header specification to drop the weighting mechanism and rely on the order of the list. Backwards compatibility be damned!

collisions with resource properties. They are included in both requests and responses.

Aside from the `Accept` header, the most common request header is probably the `Content-Type` header, which indicates the data format in which you are sending data to the server, attached to the current request. There is no negotiation to do this time around: The data is already formatted. If the server can accept the data format you've provided, it will; otherwise it should return an exception. There is no opportunity to reformat the data to fit the needs of the API.

Data

The data is just, well, data. It is a snapshot of the state (the S in REST) of the resource in question. If you are sending it to the API as an update, it represents the new state that you wish to apply to the system of record.

Responses

Status Code and Status Text

The status code is a three digit numeric code that contains a lot of information about the request and/or response. The status text is the brief message that follows the code. We'll cover status codes in detail in the best practices chapter, but for now you should know this: Incorrect status codes are the most common mistake that developers make with their REST APIs. A few of them will probably sound familiar, even if you're not a web developer: **404 Not Found**, **500 Server Error**, and **503 Server Currently Unavailable** are commonly seen by average users in web applications.

It is important that you use an appropriate status code to indicate to the client whether or not their request was acceptable, if a redirect needs to be made, if authorization is required or insufficient for the requested resource, whether there was an error, and whose fault the error was -- just to name the most common scenarios.

200 OK indicates success when reading data. **201 Created** indicates success when inserting data. **301 Moved Permanently** indicates that the client should update their links. **302 Found** indicates that a redirect is necessary but the client should *not* update their links. **400 Bad Request** is a generic error, but indicates that it was the client's fault (missing required properties, etc).

The status codes listed above only scratch the surface. The list goes on and on. I will cover these and more in much more depth in the best practices chapter. For a detailed reference, you may want to check out the Wikipedia page on HTTP Status Codes[7] or bookmark the very handy quick-reference http://httpstatus.es/. In addition, you can find a list of the most common statuses in Appendix 1.

Headers

Just as with requests, responses almost always need to include metadata specific to the server, the transmission, the request, the client, or the returned data. In the case of HTML pages, separating headers from the data has the benefit of making them appear invisible to the end user. If the response headers were included in the document body they might end up visible on the screen, which would be a poor user experience: Header metadata is intended for the programs and programmers, not the end users.

Common response headers include information about the application server that handled the request, which node in the cluster was used, metrics for querying and processing time, and more. When making REST requests from within a browser, as you are with AJAX, there are additional headers that help the browser handle the request lifecycle; including `Connection`, `Content-Encoding` (e.g. for gzip), `Date` (for caching), and so on. There are a few additional headers that we use in REST APIs to convey specific intentions and allowed behaviors, which will be covered in due time.

---

[7] http://en.wikipedia.org/wiki/List_of_HTTP_status_codes

Data

Lastly, the response usually contains some data. Hopefully, the data that the client requested, in the requested format. If not, it should either be the requested content in the default format, in the event the requested format was not available; or a description of whatever error occurred.

Why Is REST so Popular?

This is a subjective question, but a predictable one; so I'm going to answer it. Of course, my answer will be subjective too.

Common opinion tends to be cyclical. The current prevailing opinion, given the current trends in technology, tends to be that convention is (air-quotes) "better" than configuration. On this day in 2014 I happen to agree. (Writing the second edition in 2019 I still agree.) Ask me again in 10 years and my opinion may have shifted.

Conventions, when applied properly, tend to make your existing knowledge more portable. If you spend a year working with well written REST APIs, and then start a new project or get a new job and find yourself working with different REST APIs, chances are pretty good that your experience from the previous year will greatly benefit you with your new task. The URIs and the data will change, but the verbs and status codes won't.

Without conventions you need configuration. Configuration must be read, understood, and applied; by both coder and computer. SOAP's biggest flaw was that it required lengthy "contracts" describing the interactions that the client and server could have, and the acceptable way to format requests, and how responses would be formatted. This document was written in XML following the guidelines of WSDL: Web Services Description Language. As you can probably imagine, they were barely human readable, verbose, and sometimes overwhelming. This wasn't SOAP's only flaw, but it was painful enough to motivate many developers to find something better. In addition to the increased payload size of XML, the client must then process the communication contract and adhere to it, further wasting precious CPU cycles.

As the old adage goes: "Opinions are like a-holes. Everyone has one and they all stink." So does SOAP.

The next major competitor would be XML-RPC, which in some ways resembles REST APIs, but in many ways does not. Despite operating over HTTP, XML-RPC ignores the benefits of the HTTP verb, which as we've already seen is an information-dense and valuable piece of data. Instead it encourages embedding verbs in your URIs, as in `/updateWidgets`. This leads to very little conformity between APIs. Instead of being conventional, they are bespoke. As a result, your experience and knowledge of one XML-RPC api is less portable to another.

I believe that the conventions of REST also enable developers to abstract away *how things work* in their minds, and focus on *what is happening*. Less cognitive need for "how" leaves more cognitive room for "what," potentially making the developer more productive.

2: Don't Reinvent the Wheel

If you are to make use of all of the features of the metaphorical wheel that is HTTP, you need to have a good understanding of each one, individually, and in detail. Here then, is that detail.

To gain the best understanding of APIs you should familiarize yourself with implementing both API clients and API servers. We'll start with a simple REST request made with something we should all be at least casually familiar with: JavaScript – the language of the front-end web.

A Client with Which You're Already Familiar

Remember back when I said `<form>` tags are RESTful? Let's take a closer look at that. Given the following form:

```
<form method="POST" action="/bands">
    <input type="text" name="name" value="MouseRat"/>
    <input type="text" name="hometown" value="Pawnee"/>
    <button>Submit</button>
</form>
```

What happens when this form is submitted? A RESTful request. Let's look at what it looks like under the microscope. The `Content-Type` header, indicating the data-serialization used before sending the data to the server, is set to `application/x-www-form-urlencoded` and the request body contains the data in an interesting format. It resembles the query string you're familiar with from URLs containing request data in the browser, but without the leading question mark:

```
name=MouseRat&hometown=Pawnee
```

Once the request has been processed and the band data has been created, the server will usually either return a redirect (to prevent double-submission if the request should be accidentally refreshed) or some data in the response.

You've been doing REST for your whole web development career and you didn't even know it. We discussed early on how POST and GET are only the most basic of REST verbs. Can you use all of the REST verbs in form actions? As with too many things in life the answer is, "It depends."

Modern browsers are pretty good about implementing the most common verbs. You can count on GET, POST, PUT, DELETE, HEAD, OPTIONS, and maybe even PATCH to be available in the latest builds of Firefox and Chrome —maybe even modern builds of Internet Explorer, nay MS Edge!— but it wasn't always that way. Older browsers didn't support all verbs. So while it may be possible in some cases, it is definitely not something you can always count on.

Forms are not always a useful UI interaction, so let's look at a request made with more modern tools.

A Client Illustration with AJAX

To make it easier to see the important details without being distracted by the unimportant, we'll be using the popular jQuery[8] JavaScript library to abstract the tedium of making our request, and instead focus on the REST principles involved. We will make a request and then briefly discuss how you might handle the results of that request.

```
jQuery.ajax({
  url: 'https://api.example.com/v1/bands/54332'
  ,method: 'PUT'
  ,headers: {
    'Accept': 'application/json'
  }
  ,dataType: 'json'
  ,contentType: 'application/json'
  ,data: {
```

---

[8] http://jquery.com/

```
        name: 'MouseRat'
        ,members: [
            'Dwyer, Andy'
            ,'Pierson, James'
            ,'Chang, Michael'
            ,'Burlinson, Andrew "Burly"'
            ,'Rivers, Mark'
        ]
    }
})
.done(function(data, status, xhr){ /* handler */ })
.fail(function(xhr, status, err){ /* handler */ });
```

If the above code looks completely foreign to you, I recommend the JavaScript training at Codecademy[9]. It is free and takes you from absolute-zero knowledge of JavaScript to a functional beginner.

This code begins by calling a function in jQuery named `ajax` and passing it an object of options for our request. The `ajax` function executes our request asynchronously and none of our associated handler code will be executed until the request completes, returns an error, or times out. In the meantime, the `ajax` function has returned the jQuery instance, which enables us to continue calling methods on it (a process referred to as "chaining", like connecting the links in a chain), registering the success and failure callbacks. The particulars of the way this AJAX function works don't matter for this discussion. What matters is the information we are sending in the request.

The `url` attribute contains the api host (domain) and the URI ("uniform resource identifier") concatenated. You can think of the URI as a string that uniquely identifies one collection or item of data. This is our noun. Going back to the AJAX request options, the `type` attribute indicates our request verb. Note how the noun and verb

---

[9]http://www.codecademy.com/

work together to identify a discrete set of data to modify and what type of modification should be done: That's REST!

Did you notice the `/v1/` portion of the URI? You probably did, and you probably also correctly assumed that it's there to indicate which version of the API we're interested in using. When you create your own API, you're eventually going to want to change something about it; possibly breaking it for any clients still assuming it works the old way. That's where versioning comes in — but let's not get ahead of ourselves. We'll talk more about versioning when we get to best practices, in chapter 4.

The `headers` attribute sets the request headers. Note that the `Accept` header's key name in the object definition is quoted. While not strictly necessary in this case, it would be if any non alphanumeric characters —like hyphens— were used in the header name (e.g. `Content-Type`). I like to be in the habit of quoting them all for consistency and preventing bugs when an unquoted value is copied, pasted, and modified without adding the quotes when necessary. jQuery.ajax also supports an option named `contentType` which is simply shorthand for adding `Content-Type` to the headers property. That just leaves the `data` property, which contains a native object that jQuery will serialize to JSON before sending the request.

In this case our verb was `PUT` (update), so we are requesting to update the band profile for MouseRat in the bands database with the attached information. This could just as easily have been a `DELETE` request to delete the band profile, or a `GET` request to retrieve the current profile information. If you want to create a new band entry, the conventional verb+noun combination would be a `POST` to `/v1/bands` including the band profile information in the request body. Be sure to consult the API documentation to ensure its developers have not deviated from this convention.

Handling the Response

Once the server receives and processes our request, it will likely send some data back in the response. In the case of our update, it may or may not include the entire updated band profile for reference. It will also contain a status code. That status code is how jQuery decides to run the success handler (the one we registered using the `done()` method) rather than the error handler (from the `fail()` method). All 200-level (that is, 200 through 299 inclusive) would be considered successful and run the function defined in the `done()` line above. A status code in the 400 or 500 ranges indicate errors and would run the error handler defined in the `fail()` line above.

The success handler has three arguments: the data returned by the request, a text status indicator (usually just "success" and not always a copy of the HTTP response status message), and the XMLHttpRequest ("XHR") that made the request. If you would like to inspect the response metadata, you will have to dig it out of the XHR; but everything you could possibly need is contained within.

Likewise, the error handler takes three arguments, but this time in the opposite order: XHR, text status indicator (usually just "error"), and the error message (usually the HTTP response status message). Just as with the success handler, if you want more information than what is readily available in the method arguments —and you often will— you are going to have to dig it out of the XHR.

Again, these success and error handler implementations are specific to jQuery; they are used only to illustrate the request and response lifecycle, and how errors can be caught and handled in a non-disruptive way for the users of your applications.

Just as before, this is not intended as the end-all, be-all of REST request references. It is meant only to illustrate how the most fundamental aspects of REST coalesce into a concise and meaningful request. If you are writing a REST client in a language other than JavaScript —because remember: REST is not just for web servers and web-browsers (clients) to talk to one another— the syntax might look different; but the concepts will remain the same.

You will specify your HTTP verb and the URL at which it should be directed. You may need to include some headers and request data.

And when the API returns a response, you need to parse it to find out what the server did with your request, if anything.

Designing Your Own API

By now you have a pretty solid high-level understanding of each element of a REST API. Now it is time to get into the nitty-gritty details of each element, so that you can anticipate and properly handle each when your clients inquire about them.

Whatever your back-end language, it (hopefully) has some tools for obtaining the raw HTTP request details, or possibly even REST-friendly frameworks. Once you have the tools and know the concepts, the rest is implementation details.

Know Your Verbs

`GET` is for reading, `POST` is for creating, `PUT` is for updating, and `DELETE` is for deleting. These are the four basic verbs used with REST. But they are far from everything.

In addition, we have `PATCH`, which is like `PUT` but allows for partial updating; `HEAD`, which is like `GET` but only the headers are returned; and `OPTIONS` which is used to pre-flight a request to make sure it doesn't violate any security restrictions. We'll discuss `OPTIONS` more in the security chapter.

Use Sensible Nouns

This will be covered in greater detail when we get to Best Practices, but repetition helps drive the point home, right? Your nouns should be descriptive. If a natural key[10] exists, use that to uniquely identify your data. Often in situations where a natural key does not exist, it is preferable to use some near-unique data in combination with a surrogate key[11]. `/users/John-Smith-42691`

---

[10] A uniquely identifying characteristic that occurs naturally in the data and has a logical relationship to the data.

[11] A unique value generated for the purpose of identifying a record: An auto-incrementing integer and a GUID are common examples.

is better than /users/42691 because it will be useful to developers in debugging and other scenarios when they may be reading and comparing data. Of course it doesn't make a lick of difference to the client code, but we don't write APIs strictly for other programs: People are our clients too.

Know when to use Query String Parameters

App servers don't always allow GET requests to have a body, but sometimes you need to add additional metadata to your request. Some things are appropriate to embed into the URI (/users/John-Smith-42691), and some things are not (/users?page=3). What should you include in the URI? Only the things that are *required* to identify the record(s) in question. Anything else is optional and should not be considered part of the URI. Include optional parameters in the query string instead.

Remember, the URL is made up of several pieces; and the query string is not part of the URI.

    protocol://hostname/uri/uri?querystring

Request and Response Data Formatting

You may be lucky enough to get away with all JSON input and all JSON output. Not everyone can. You may need to be able to handle XML or other data input and output formats, too. Be prepared to do content negotiation, as described in the first chapter.

You should also be aware of a trend that, to the best of my knowledge, started in the Ruby on Rails community. Instead of sending an Accept header to specify that the client wants JSON data back, the API may accept a ".json" suffix on the URI to indicate that it would like JSON back: /widgets.json. While this does make it easier to explore and test APIs directly from a browser window, it also has the potential to complicate your API's routing table.

Status Codes are Crucial

Memorize the most common status codes, and use them judiciously. Keep a handy[12] reference for the rest of them[13]. You will be referencing it frequently.

- 200 Success

- 404 Not Found

- 500 Server Error

- 400 Client Error (malformed request, missing required property, etc)

- 401 Not Authorized (I don't know who you are)

- 403 Forbidden (I know who you are, and that's why I can't let you do that)

Technically, according to the spec, status 401 implies more than, "I don't know who you are." You are expected to return the header `WWW-Authenticate: Basic` with it, to indicate that the client should retry their request with HTTP Basic Authentication headers included. If you're using something other than HTTP Basic Auth for your API, what should you do? Should you use a different status code (make one up?) to indicate the same thing only without the requirement of Basic Auth in the response; or should you blaze ahead waving the standards zealot away with a brush of your hand? That is for you to decide.

My personal opinion is to just use 401 anyway. It seems to me that the standards simply neglected to predict authentication mechanisms beyond Basic Auth, or they would have allowed a more flexible response.

---

[12] http://httpstatus.es/

[13] http://en.wikipedia.org/wiki/List_of_HTTP_status_codes

Don't Forget the Status Message

While there are conventional messages that go with the most common status codes, there is nothing stopping you from customizing them. If `200 Update Accepted` suits your needs better than `200 OK` then go for it. For a quick laugh, look up the standard status message for status 418.

There you have it, the basics of REST APIs. If you get these right, all that remains is minor details.

3: Security

Write enough APIs and sooner or later you are going to have to secure one. There are different challenges you might face in securing your API, and the more complex your security needs are, the more complex the solution tends to be.

Basic Auth over SSL

The most basic option for securing your API is to use the security baked into HTTP. If it satisfies your needs, don't reinvent the wheel, right?

Basic Auth is the simplest technique for applying access control to any resource on the internet, REST APIs included, because it does not require a login form, sessions, or cookies. The server returns a flag that tells the client that basic authentication is required, and the client then knows that a username and password must be sent in the request headers of subsequent requests.

If a request is made without the `Authorization` header when basic auth is required, the server should respond with status code `401 Unauthorized` and the header `WWW-Authenticate: Basic realm="Some Realm String"`. It is expected that, assuming the client has or can somehow obtain a valid account, it should repeat the previous request with the header `Authorization: Basic c2tyb29iOjEyMzQ1`.

But where does this `Authorization` header value come from, and what the heck is the realm that is mentioned in the `WWW-Authenticate` challenge? The authorization header is made up of two things: The authorization method ("Basic", same as issued in the challenge), and the base64-encoded username and password. The username and password are concatenated with a colon between them, as in: `username:password` and then the resulting string is base64 encoded. The realm is sort of a namespace for the authentication challenge. It is a free-form string, and is a method

21

whereby the web server may group together web resources that will accept the same authorization account. It is expected that any account valid for one resource in the "ABC" realm is valid for all resources in that realm; though not necessarily for all realms on the same domain. You might think of it like a single-sign-on descriptor: Any API using the same realm should accept the same credentials.

Because base64 encoding is *not* encryption and is easily decoded, this is no more secure than sending usernames and passwords in plain text; which I hope you already know is a patently bad idea. That does not mean you should avoid basic auth, it means that you should only use it in conjunction with SSL or TLS.

Externally Provisioned API Keys

If you can't or won't use basic auth over SSL/TLS, the next simplest option would be externally provisioned API keys. An API key is simply a sufficiently-unguessable identifier that uniquely identifies one entity to whom you are granting access. If that sounds vague, that's because it is: You can use anything you want. You could use integers if you wanted, but they would be pretty straight forward to guess or brute-force, which makes them insecure. More commonly you see SHA hashes or GUIDs used.

What does one do with an API key? Simple: Include it with every request. For `GET`, `DELETE`, and any other requests where the request body may not be inspected, that means it should go in a query string parameter:

```
GET /widgets?apikey=h4923jdh7843hd32h
```

For `POST`, `PUT`, or other requests that usually include a body, you can include it in the body:

```
{ "apikey":"h4923jdh7843hd32h" }
```

I am drawing a distinction here between "api keys" and "externally-provisioned api keys" because inline authenticated API keys are next. By externally-provisioned I mean that they are assigned and available out-of-band from the API.

By using an externally provisioned API key, you gain the ability to assign more than one key to a given consumer, and you can revoke a key at any time to block its user's access to the API without fear that the legitimate account has been compromised because the user's account credentials have not been transmitted in any API requests. It is still advisable to use SSL/TLS in this scenario to mask the URL and request arguments, including the API key. Just because it isn't the user's password does not mean it wouldn't be useful to an attacker. If it grants extra permissions it is just as good as their password, so protect it like they are one and the same.[14]

Inline Login that Provisions a Key

Just as with externally provisioned keys, inline login has the benefit that you may, if you wish, assign multiple keys to a single account. If someone logs into your service, via your API, on both their iPhone and iPad, you can include the device id in the authentication request. The API may then use that id to determine whether to return an existing key in the case of a known device, or a new key in the case of a new device. Also like externally provisioned keys, they can be easily revoked at any time to block an abusive consumer. However one key difference from externally provisioned keys is that the user's credentials *have* been transmitted over the internet. If you believe that an api key is being abused, you should revoke that key and reset the user's password as well — it may be compromised too.

You should choose inline login and key provisioning in situations when you are unable to provide a key via out-of-band methods (perhaps your app is device-only, there is no website component); or when transposing or copying and pasting it into the API consumer would be difficult or impractical. This is why many mobile apps tend to just ask you for your username and password, rather than have you setup an API key on their website and copy it into their mobile app.

---

[14]Not to mention that SSL Certificates are now available for free from reputable services like LetsEncrypt and Cloudflare.

Just as with externally provisioned keys, these requests should always be sent over SSL/TLS to mask the api key as well as the URL and the rest of the request and response data from any would-be attackers monitoring the traffic. Are we sensing a theme, here? Pretty much all API traffic, for anything even remotely sensitive, should be sent over SSL/TLS, at a minimum.

Since authentication does not map directly to an HTTP method and we're eschewing HTTP basic auth, I like to think of authentication requests as the creation (POST) of a new API key:

```
POST /apikeys
Accept: application/json


{ "username":"skroob", "password":"12345" }
```

To which the API might respond:

```
201 Created
Content-Type: application/json


{ "apikey":"c3Vycm91bmRlZCBieSBhc3Nob2xlcw" }
```

JSON Web Tokens (JWT)

JSON Web Tokens ("JWT") came about in late 2010. They have since become a popular mechanism for identifying users, sharing some attributes about them and "claims" of certain permissions, and –crucially– validating that those attributes and claims are authentically provided by the provider of the JWT.

The information contained in a JWT is not considered "secret." It is not encrypted, even though it might appear so at first glance. Just like Basic Auth over SSL, the payload is only Base64 encoded to ensure it is composed of a consistent and safe set of characters no matter what its content contains; and Base64 encoding is trivial to decode without any sort of key. This isn't material to the discussion, but it's an easy mistake to make so I want to provide that clarification to any

JWT newbies that might be reading this. Don't put something inside the payload of a JWT thinking it is safe from prying eyes.

You can read all about the structure and composition of JWTs at https://jwt.io, but for our purposes, I'll explain why I don't think they are a good fit for REST API authentication in most cases.

First, a JWT expires at a set date and time, and you can't expire it early; if, for example, the key leaks and needs to be replaced. A leaked key is fair game to anyone who would like to use it until it expires. As a side effect of this behavior, best practices generally suggest that you create short-lived JWTs so that they have to be refreshed often, giving you the opportunity to decline to refresh them, should you want to. By contrast, you can simply delete an API key record from your database/cache/etc, and no future requests authenticated by that key will succeed.

Second, you have the added code, responsibility, and resource-costs of providing the mechanism for refreshing them. Think of refreshing the token as a sort of login-lite. You're allowing the old JWT to be exchanged for a new, updated token. These things are worth doing if you're only using JWT for benefits that you can't get elsewhere, but when there are better alternatives (like all of the options described in this chapter!) it simply doesn't make sense to jump through these hoops.

Finally, API keys are typically expected to live anywhere from weeks to months. An expiration that long on a JWT might be considered downright dangerous. Not only are you burdening *yourself* with the regular refreshes, but the user, too. If they don't want their JWT to expire, they need to refresh it regularly.

In my opinion any of the other mechanisms described in this chapter would be a better choice for securing the average API.

If it seems like I've chosen my words carefully to say that JWT is a bad fit for many APIs but possibly good for others, that's because I have. So what use cases might it be good for?

The primary strength of a JWT is that it can contain the list of permissions that you want to grant ("claims"), and you can trust it because of the signature. If you have a particularly extensive API and want to have fine-grained control over which URI's are accessible to which users, you could include the list of allowable URI's in the payload and trust that the user hasn't tampered with it because if they had then the signature would no longer match.

Another potential problem that JWT might help you solve is horizontal scaling. If your API sees so much traffic that you're load balancing it across multiple servers and you don't want to cache the api key lookups for all active users in the memory of every server, then JWT helps you offload that authorization to a trustworthy, stateless source.

As with every problem, there are multiple solutions. By knowing the strengths and weaknesses of each you can choose the one best suited to your strengths and your limitations.

OAuth

OAuth[15] is a hairy beast that has filled many books on its own — there were no less than eight available on Amazon.com in December of 2014— so there is no possible way I can do it complete justice in one short chapter of this short book. But I will explain what problems it solves and give you a basic understanding of how it solves them, so that if it is the right solution for your needs, you know what to read up on next.

The problem that OAuth seeks to solve is delegation of privileges to a 3rd party. Thus far I have written about APIs in the sense that there were only two parties involved: the API provider, and the API consumer. But what do you do when your app becomes popular and people want to develop 3rd party applications that make use of your API on behalf of other users? You need a system that allows those users to grant permission on an ad-hoc and individual basis to any

---

[15] http://oauth.net/

application they choose, and to revoke that access on-demand from within your application; and that allows the applications to act on behalf of users that have delegated some permissions to them. That's what OAuth is for.

There are three parties involved: The API, the user, and the delegate. E.g. The Twitter API, you as a Twitter user, and the app that you want to use to read and post to Twitter on your behalf.

The delegation process usually works like this: The user indicates to the delegate that they want to use the delegate. The delegate forwards the user's browser to a screen in your api/application, with parameters indicating the user-delegation relationship that is desired. The user, who has an active session or is prompted to log in, is given the opportunity to approve or deny the request. If the request is approved, some security tokens are generated and usually sent separately to the delegate, and the user is redirected back to the delegate. Having already received the security tokens, the delegate is prepared to act on behalf of the user, and can allow them into the application and start making API requests to create, read, update, and delete their data.

In a way, OAuth is a system for managing delegation of an API key to a trusted 3rd party. There's a little more to it than that, but at the end of the day, the delegate has an api key they can use to act on your behalf.

In addition to requiring the generated security tokens in subsequent API requests, the API also requires that all requests be "signed." Signing involves listing all of the data properties to be included in the request, and their values, as well as identifying information about the 3rd party application and the user it is representing, and then hashing this data with a one-way hash like HMAC-SHA1 using a pre-determined secret signing key (one of the security tokens previously sent to the delegate). The resulting signature is added to the request as an additional header. When the request is being parsed by the API, its contents are run through the same signing process and the signatures are compared. If they match then it can be safely assumed that the request was not tampered with between the time it was sent and the time the API received it. Also note that this process does not require decryption. The same one-way encryption is done by both the delegate and the API and the signatures are compared.

OAuth also requires SSL, as a rule. If it's not transmitted over SSL, it's not OAuth.

Cross Origin Resource Sharing

In addition to authentication, another security concern you should be aware of is Cross Origin Resource Sharing, or CORS. It specifically concerns AJAX requests made from web browsers, but a significant amount of REST is done in this exact context so when creating an API it is something you should be prepared to discuss and possibly support.

Modern browsers implement what is called the same-origin policy[16], to protect the user. Without it, any malicious website could make XHR requests to websites that you are logged into, and they would appear to be legitimate requests coming from you. To protect against this type of attack, the same-origin policy requires that in order to access resources on a domain, the script must originate from the same domain.

Unfortunately, in this context "originate" means that the **page** containing the `<script></script>` tag is served from the same domain, *not* that the **script** is served from that domain; and this is why the same-origin policy does not protect from cross-site scripting (XSS) attacks. Practically speaking, what this means is that if you are able to trick Facebook into embedding a `<script></script>` tag of your own design, you can access people's Facebook data, including their cookies. This was the source of several "worms" that were more common in the early days of Facebook, Twitter, MySpace, etc. However, putting a malicious `<script></script>` tag on your

---

[16]http://en.wikipedia.org/wiki/Same-origin_policy

own website that attempts to access unauthorized data from the Facebook API *will* be thwarted by the same-origin policy: The browser won't even let the request be sent because of the domain mismatch.

The browser makes this decision by performing what is known as a pre-flight request. Pre-flighting is a copy of the intended request, with the verb changed to `OPTIONS` and the request body (if any) stripped and the intended request headers enumerated in a special header. The server responds to this `OPTIONS` request with some special headers that indicate which verbs are allowed, which headers are allowed, and which domains ("origins") are allowed. If any of the intended request parameters would violate these restrictions, the request is canceled by the browser before it is ever sent.

Server-to-server communication is not subject to the same-origin policy, and thus making `OPTIONS` requests is not strictly required or enforced. However if you intend to allow AJAX requests to your API, even when not running on a traditional domain (e.g. in a Cordova/Phonegap powered mobile application), CORS matters to you. Here is what you need to do to support it.

Access-Control-Allow-Origin

The pre-flight request will contain a header named `Origin` which names the domain making the request. If you want to allow the request to continue, return the same origin value in your response in the `Access-Control-Allow-Origin` header.

Request:
```
Origin: https://example.com
```

Response:
```
Access-Control-Allow-Origin: https://example.com
```

Alternatively, if you want to globally enable CORS (unsafe, be careful!), simply return an asterisk:

```
Access-Control-Allow-Origin: *
```

Access-Control-Allow-Methods

This `OPTIONS` response header is straight forward: Based on the requested URI, return a simple comma-delimited list of allowed verbs in the header `Access-Control-Allow-Methods`. If the requested resource allows `GET`, `POST`, and `PUT`, but not `DELETE`, the response would be as follows. Don't forget to include `OPTIONS`, as some clients will take its exclusion to mean that CORS is disabled.

```
Access-Control-Allow-Methods: GET,POST,PUT,OPTIONS
```

Access-Control-Allow-Headers

Lastly, you must also explicitly allow all of the intended request headers if you want to allow the request to continue. It could be confusing if the intended-request's headers were sent as the headers of the pre-flight request, so instead they are sent in a comma-delimited list as the pre-flight request header `Access-Control-Request-Headers`. I have yet to find a case where I needed to deny a request solely based on a desired request header, so my general approach has been to parrot back all of the headers listed here, as well as a standard set. In addition to any additional headers listed in `Access-Control-Request-Headers`, I always list the following:

```
Origin, Authorization, X-CSRF-Token, X-Requested-
With, Content-Type, X-HTTP-Method-Override, Accept,
Referrer, User-Agent
```

Of course, if you have good reason to refuse requests based on any headers listed here or that you expect clients may send, exclude it from `Access-Control-Allow-Headers`.

JSONP

Another way around the same-origin policy is to use JSONP. This practice takes advantage of the fact that JSON data can be evaluated to become JavaScript data, and through the use of a special request parameter, wraps the response data in a function-call. The URL that generates the wrapped response is then embedded into the page as a script tag at runtime. Once the response has downloaded, it is executed like any other script include would be; thereby calling the response handler function and passing it the response data. In this way, it is functionally equivalent to loading an image or script file from another domain, as far as the browser is concerned, and is nothing for it to be worried about.

JSONP can be very handy, but does come with its own limitations. To start, you can only make GET requests. Even if you could use method tunneling of some sort, it is a bad idea to tunnel an unsafe verb through a safe verb, because you never know what intermediaries and oddball browsers will do with it. Because of this, JSONP is typically reserved for data-loading only — no modifications. Further, you can not send HTTP headers (remember, you're just adding a <script></script> tag to the document at runtime). This gives you very limited ability to specify what you want and how you want it.

Typically a JSONP request uses the query string parameter named `jsonp` to indicate the function name that you would like the response wrapped in. If you were to make a JSONP request to GET / musketeers/1, it might look like this:

```
<script src="example.com/musketeers/1?
jsonp=handle"></script>
```

The response would be the requested data, in JSON format, wrapped with the requested method name; in this case `handle`:

```
handle({"name":"D'Artagnan"});
```

JSONP's inability to send custom headers precludes it from using basic auth or OAuth bearer tokens. It is possible to use an OAuth `access_token` as a query parameter instead, but it should be noted that many http servers log query parameters by default, so the `access_token` approach is less secure, even if done over SSL. JSONP helps break down the high barriers setup by browsers when you don't need them, but in doing so sacrifices some ability to be secure.

4: Best Practices

No writing about REST is complete without a list of best practices. As I have noted a few times, the REST community is rife with disagreement, but at the end of the day what matters is that you are getting important work done. Whether or not you get the official Roy Fielding— or Hacker News Commenters— or Some Guy That Wrote A Book Seal of Approval is tertiary at best.

What follows are my opinions on what make pragmatic best practices, after years of practical work shipping REST APIs and clients that use them. Much of my earlier work violated some of the rules I include here, and I either learned the hard way, or got lucky but eventually came around. Some of these fly in the face of modern popular opinion, but I believe that their pragmatism will stand the test of time.

Not Everything Maps Neatly to a Noun

What if your API launches an assault of quad-copters to attack your coworkers with Nerf darts? Is that a POST or a PUT? Or something else?

I imagine the nuance of every possible use case could result in a different answer, but if we have to arrive at a general rule of thumb, my gut says go with POST for most things that don't obviously fit elsewhere. You are **creating** that quadcopter assault, and if the same request was submitted again —presumably— another assault would be launched. That means that the action is *not* idempotent, and is instead unsafe.[17]

Technically RFC 7231[18] gives you permission to create your own methods (verbs), though it does require that you register them with

---

[17] Someone could lose an eye!

[18] http://tools.ietf.org/html/rfc7231#section-4.1

the HTTP method registry.[19] Unfortunately, your custom methods may not be supported by intermediate proxies, which may deny or rewrite the request (e.g. assume it is a `GET` or a `POST`) or even cache its results, preventing similar or duplicate requests from being sent. Custom methods are simultaneously an insanely good idea and a dangerous game to play. I just skip them and map to traditional verbs as best as I can.

Status Codes Are Your Friend

Most developers are familiar with a handful of common status codes: 200 means everything went as expected; 404 means not found; 500 means there was a server error; and you may also be familiar with 503, when the web server layer is unable to communicate with the application server layer for one reason or another. But did you know that there are more than twenty that you should be prepared to send or receive at any given time?

Success Statuses

201 Created indicates that your data-creation request was successful, and is usually paired with some combination of headers:

- `Location: http://...` indicates the new URL for the created resource

- `X-Inserted-ID: 42` indicates just the id value of the created resource

X-headers —headers that begin with an `X-` prefix— are usually custom headers defined by the developer, and not standardized. You may see many of them in your career, so now you know why they are prefixed.

202 Accepted is much like 201, but indicates that the creation has not yet completed — perhaps it is asynchronous and still queued. Unless the application code is in charge of assigning new id values, it

---

[19] http://www.iana.org/assignments/http-methods/http-methods.xhtml

33

will not be possible to include the `Inserted-ID` and `Location` headers in the response.

204 No Content indicates that the request was successful, like a 200, but that there is no content coming with the response, because it is not necessary.

Redirection Statuses

Most web developers are familiar with 301 and 302. **301 Moved Permanently** indicates that if the URI is cached (e.g. in google's indexes) that the cache should be updated to the value provided in the `Location` header of the response. **302 Found** indicates that the client will need to make a request to the value provided in the `Location` header, but that it *should not* update any cached URI information. There are some subtle differences between 302 and 303, which is similar, but many pre-HTTP/1.1 browsers do not understand 303, so it is common and acceptable to use a 302 instead. This is why it is common to return a 302 after a form post: to ask the browser to request another URL without risking having spiders forget about the referring page.

304 Not Modified indicates that the caching checksum/hash/etc provided with the request is still valid, so there is no reason for the client to re-download the requested data again. This will be covered in more depth in the upcoming section on caching.

Client-Error Statuses

400 Bad Request is a general purpose catch-all for client errors. "It's not me, it's you!" If the client did something wrong, and there is not a more appropriate status code to use, then use 400.

401 Unauthorized indicates that the API supports authentication, but you have yet to make use of it. "I don't know who you are."

402 Payment Required was reserved for future use and is self explanatory: The API in question relates to a paid service, and the user —who has successfully authenticated to identify themselves— owes you money, so their API access is cut off. It's odd that this is still "reserved" after all of these years, but if you're going to require payments to use your API, you might as well use this status when applicable.

403 Forbidden indicates that the authenticated user does not have permission to perform the requested action. "I know who you are, and you're not allowed to do that." Note the distinction from 401. In the case of a 401, it is possible that resubmitting the request with the proper authentication information could allow it to proceed. In the case of a 403, the specified user should not retry the request unless they change their authentication credentials to act on behalf of a different user.

404 Not Found indicates that the requested resource can not be found in the system. Many REST newbies stumble on this point. Supposing we have an API with a `/widgets` resource and at least one member; should `GET /wigdets/1` (with the g and d transposed) return a 404? Should `GET /widgets/42` (where widgets is correctly spelled, but id 42 has not been created) return a 404? In both cases, the answer is yes. Remember that computers are relatively dumb, at least in that they only know as much as we tell them. A request to `/wigdets` is functionally equivalent to a request to `/XYZ` when you have not defined that resource either. Misspellings, though common, are not easily detected and corrected in an automated fashion. Whatever your API uses for routing will likely return a 404 if it can't find a matching route (as would be the case with `/wigdets`), and you should return 404 for `/widgets/42` if it doesn't exist yet, too.

405 Method Not Allowed indicates that the URI matches a known route, but that the requested method, or verb, is not implemented. This will probably be handled for you by your REST API tooling or framework. This status code is distinct from 403 in that *nobody* is allowed to perform the request, as a handler has not been implemented.

406 Not Acceptable indicates that the resource was found, but that it can not be delivered with the content-type defined in the request's `Accept` header. The client may either repeat the request with a suitable `Accept` header, or not repeat it at all.

409 Conflict indicates that the request can not be completed because of a conflict. If you are allowing clients to insert data with a `PUT` and specifying their own id values, you can use 409 to indicate that their specified id is taken. Alternatively, if you use ETags (as described in the upcoming section on caching), clients can indicate the version of the data on which they have based their changes. If an update `PUT` request arrives and the current value of the data does not match the version code (ETag) included in the request, then the record was updated by a 3rd party between the client's `GET` and `PUT` requests, and the `PUT` request is being rejected for being out of sync.

410 Gone indicates that the requested resource *used to* be available, but is now gone, and that there is no plan to bring it back. This exists as a way to allow spiders to clean up their records; though implementing it can be difficult to automate. It is uncommon to use this status, but not unheard of.

420 Enhance Your Calm — no, not a joke; at least not on my part. This status was introduced by Twitter and is now very popularly used to indicate that you will soon exceed the rate limit if you do not decrease the frequency of your requests. Additionally **429 Too Many Requests** indicates that you have exceeded the rate limit.

Server-Error Statuses

Just as 400 was a generic catch-all for client errors, **500 Server Error** is a generic catch-all for server errors. Any error that may not be laid at the feet of the client should have a status code in the 500-range. If no specific 5xx status is available, 500 will do the job.

501 Not Implemented indicates that the server doesn't recognize the method at all. While RFC 7231 gives you permission to create your own methods, that does not mean that all servers will instantly understand what your new method is or how it should be implemented.

503 Service Unavailable indicates that the web server layer is functioning but that an application server that would be used to process the request is not. This often indicates an application server crash. Generally this is not something you will need to code for in your APIs, but possibly will need to handle in your clients.

509 Bandwidth Limit Exceeded is not defined by any RFC, but is implemented by many http servers. In a situation where a single API serves content on behalf of multiple 3rd parties and each party has a limited amount of bandwidth, when that bandwidth is exhausted the API should return status 509.

On top of all of the status codes described here, there are even more, and most of them are opaque and arcane; reminiscent of strange technologies or problems of yesteryear. If you have a good grasp on the statuses defined above, you should do just fine.

Cache, and Enable Caching Where Appropriate

It should go without saying: A fast API is a happy API. Your API should make a reasonable effort to return results as quickly as possible. Often that means some level of server-side caching for `GET` requests. Only you can decide what is appropriate for your API, but chances are good some level of server caching is a good idea. You can generally use the same server-side caching mechanisms in an API that you would in a regular web application.

Client caching is relatively easy for you to support and enables your clients to decide what type of caching they want to do, and how aggressively they want to do it. The three most common client caching techniques are the `Last-Modified` header, the `Expires` header, and the `ETag` header.

The first two are fairly self-explanatory. You specify the date and time that the requested data was last modified, or that the API considers it expired. The former allows the client to decide how fresh it wants its cache to be, and the latter gives the API the opportunity to suggest to the client how soon it should check for updates. These dates should be returned using the **HTTP Date** format specified in

RFC 7231[20], and resemble: `Last-Modified: Mon, 01 Dec 2014 12:34:56 GMT`. Paired with the `HEAD` verb, these headers can provide a good way to verify that the data should be requested before requesting it.

ETags are ever so slightly more complex. Any opaque unique string may be returned, but it is common to use a cryptographic hash like MD5 or SHA1 of the entirety of the response data:

```
GET /widgets
```

To which the API responds:

```
200 OK
ETag: 1945FB1537B4F4AB6F4C5FEAD1B0D839

[ some, widgets ]
```

On subsequent requests for the same resource, the client may recognize that it has an ETag value available from a previous request, and send it in an `If-None-Match` request header:

```
GET /widgets
If-None-Match: 1945FB1537B4F4AB6F4C5FEAD1B0D839
```

The server analyzes the widgets data collection, and realizing that the data has not changed since the last time it was requested (because the ETag value would be the same), and wanting to save itself the bandwidth and the client some time, it returns 304 instead of 200, and omits the data:

```
304 Not Modified
```

Seeing this, the client goes about its business using the data it already had in its local cache instead of downloading updates from the API.

Sometimes you want to require that a resource *has not changed*. When updating a record you may ensure that there were no changes made by a 3rd party between the time the record was last retrieved

---

[20]http://tools.ietf.org/html/rfc7231

and the time the PUT request is sent by having the client send the ETag header value back in an `If-Match` header

```
PUT /widgets/42
If-Match: 1945FB1537B4F4AB6F4C5FEAD1B0D839

{ ... }
```

The API should only accept the update if the current data's ETag matches the value listed in the request. If the current ETag value differs from the one in the request, the API should return a status 409:

```
409 Conflict


{ "errors": [ "Base state is out of date; update refused." ] }
```

Not all APIs implement this behavior, so you can not assume that it will be present in every API with which you work.

There are other headers that your API may implement support for: `Cache-Control` tells the client and proxies how long (in seconds) a response may be cached for; and `If-Modified-Since` works similarly to `If-None-Match` but by using the `Last-Modified` date instead of the ETag value. These are less commonly used and in the case of `Cache-Control` being replaced by CDNs and hardware vendors with dynamic caching features.

All of the above applies regardless of what kind of client is involved. Web browsers, mobile browsers, native mobile devices, and other servers should all have the capability to use caching headers to their advantage.

Implement HEAD

The `HEAD` verb is a hidden gem of HTTP. It asks your API to respond with the same headers that would come with an otherwise-identical `GET` request, but no response body at all. Especially when a data payload is large or irregularly updated, having the ability to inspect the response headers without requesting all of the data can save a lot of bandwidth and make the API appear faster.

Allow HTTP Method Tunneling

We have already established that not all browsers, proxies, and firewalls support all HTTP Verbs (for shame!)... So what can you do about this? HTTP method tunneling is the ability to pass the intended verb as a header value instead of as the HTTP method. The header name is X-HTTP-Method-Override, and typically it is paired with POST because of its unsafe status and prolific availability.

```
POST /widgets/42
X-HTTP-Method-Override: DELETE
```

Because of the limited availability of PUT and DELETE, the above request would be likely to be a supported way to make your DELETE requests.

I would like to say that modern browsers and hardware are making this limitation exceedingly rare, and that may very well be a true statement, but there is no way to know for sure that the server or client you are connecting to is not behind a circa 1995 proxy in the basement of some underfunded University somewhere. It is true that modern browsers have good support for all standard HTTP verbs, but it is not yet true that we can reasonably expect all users to be using modern versions of their browser. Unfortunately, this limitation must remain on our minds, for now.

Version Your API from Day One

Nothing is completely stable. Change is inevitable. We can expect that for any reasonably useful API there will eventually be a second version (which is not to say Version 2). This best practice argues that you should include a version in your API even with its first public release, for a few reasons.

That you should version your API from the outset is fairly well accepted at this point, but the technique that you use to specify the version is still hotly contested. There are three major schools of thought: Version as part of the `Accept` header, Version in a custom header, and Version as part of the URI. Each has its pros and cons.

The `Accept` header approach keeps your URIs extra clean and can, depending on your architecture, make it easier (or harder!) to maintain the multiple versions going forward. It is extreme adherence to the philosophy of semantic URIs, and true faith that the `Accept` header should describe the "nature" of the data you are requesting, that should lead you to choose this method. In this case, instead of a simple `Accept: application/json` header, they become more complex: `Accept: application/vnd.myApplication.v1+json`. If you go this route, you have instantly given up the simplicity of sending someone a link to click. Instead anyone wishing to use the API must carefully construct a request with complicated headers.

The custom header approach (e.g. `API-Version: v1`, or whatever else you may choose to name it) seeks to gain the benefits of the `Accept` header approach while shrugging off the added complexity. Again, depending on your architecture, it may accomplish these goals. However, for what it accomplishes in semantic URIs and comparative simplicity over the `Accept` header approach, it still fails the share-a-link test, and is no longer truly semantic, as you have eschewed the HTTP-provided mechanism for describing the desired "nature" of the data being requested.

The URI approach cedes some semantic correctness in the URI, but in exchange it achieves extreme simplicity: `/v1/widgets/42`. You can easily share a link to any version of the data, no special headers required. I favor this approach —though I won't try to tell you that any one of them is "better" than the others— because it is easily explained, easily tested, and easily maintained by simply copying the existing code into a new folder. There may be slightly more code duplication with this approach but only by a small margin, as two versions of the same route handler still need to exist when the same codebase handles all versions.

41

When to Bump Versions

There are two things you may find yourself doing to your API over its lifetime:

- Adding additional routes, features, response properties, etc.

- Breaking backwards compatibility

It is not always necessary to increase the version number if you add additional routes, features, properties, etc; though if you make *significant* additions, you might want to anyway, just to indicate that there was significant change.

If you break backwards compatibility, you **must** bump the version number. That includes changing routes, adding required parameters, removing or renaming response properties, etc. If you expect to evolve your API a lot over its lifetime, you may want to consider using SemVer[21], which describes a standard method for embedding a bit more semantic context in your version numbers.

Default to the First Version

If you made the mistake of not including a version indicator with the first public release of your API and there are any dependents of it, you may find yourself wondering how to handle requests that do not specify a version after adding your second version. The short answer is that you should default to the first version.

Some might argue that requests without a specific version should always return the most recent version, but this has the potential to break people's implementations that depend on your API. You could make the case that developers might want to always default to the bleeding edge release of your API in their development environment, to which I would counter that this is only acceptable if the decision predates the initial release or first dependent of your API.

---

[21]http://semver.org

Instead, I would recommend that you still default unversioned requests to use the first version, and provide an alias that always points to the max version for anyone that might want to always ride on the bleeding edge release.

Paginate Large Datasets

Nobody wants to wait for 2mb of data to download over a cell phone 3g connection, and in fact during this download many users will begin to question whether the app in question has broken. For this reason it is best to paginate any dataset that is or is likely to become large. There are two aspects to pagination: How to request a specific page, and how to indicate page availability.

Pagination filters should be applied through query string parameters: `/widgets?page=4&pageSize=100`. An alternative to the numbered pages approach is often necessary with temporal data. Twitter's API supports `since_id` and `before_id` filters for seeking forward and backward in time, respectively; because by the time you can select and parse a page of data, more has usually been created and the records from page 1 would now be split between pages 1 and 2.

Additionally you must decide how you will indicate to your consumers when there are additional pages available. GitHub's API is often heralded for many reasons, pagination among them. With an average request, they might return a `Link` header like the following:

```
Link: <https://api.github.com/search/code?
q=addClass+user%3Amozilla&page=3>; rel="next",

<https://api.github.com/search/code?
q=addClass+user%3Amozilla&page=34>; rel="last",

<https://api.github.com/search/code?
q=addClass+user%3Amozilla&page=1>; rel="first",

<https://api.github.com/search/code?
q=addClass+user%3Amozilla&page=1>; rel="prev"
```

This is an example of a concept known as Hypermedia As The Engine Of Application State, something we will discuss in more detail in the next chapter. The idea is that the response includes information about possible next steps: in this case, additional pages that might be of interest. GitHub provides links to the first, last, next, and previous pages in an easily parsed format.

One alternative to this approach would be to embed similar information or links into the data response, which is considered an anti-pattern because it is a degree of reinventing the wheel (see: Avoid Data Envelopes, below).

Another alternative is to write some documentation. If your API is implemented with consistent methodologies then a little bit of simple documentation can go a long way.

Be Consistent in Your URIs

What kind of identifiers will you use? Natural keys? Surrogate keys? Integers? Guids? A non-unique data point combined with a surrogate key (e.g. `Tuttle-Adam-42`)? Whatever you pick, be as consistent between resources as is reasonable. Don't switch back and forth on a whim. As a general rule of thumb I give priority to natural keys, falling back to a combined natural-non-unique & surrogate key, for the increased human readability —as I find this makes it easier to keep things straight in my head in debugging sessions— but sometimes you need obfuscation. Maybe you don't want to let on how many records there are in a set for some reason. In that case Guids may prove useful, and I don't think there is anything wrong with using them exclusively for these niche cases, making them inconsistent with the rest of your API. As long as you can back up your decisions with solid reasoning, do what you think is best!

When naming data collections, use a consistent pluralization. Either use singular, or use plural, but don't mix. I tend to prefer plural, because I like to think of collections as directories of a file system (`/widgets`) and members as files in a directory (`/widgets/my-widget`). But you could say I have a cognitive dissonance on this topic, too, as I tend to prefer singular table names in my databases.

Only things that are *absolutely necessary* to identify a specific resource belong in the URI. Everything else —filters, sorting, pagination, etc— should be query string parameters.

Relationship Nesting

Early in your API design career it is tempting to nest relationships deeply: `/authors/Tuttle-Adam-42/books/REST-Assured/reviews/43437289`. There are a couple of schools of thought on the matter, and neither one of them is more right than the other. One side says that nothing should be more than two levels deep: `/authors/tuttle-adam-42` and `/books/REST-Assured`; while the other side says some level of nesting is acceptable, but most can't quantify what nesting would be acceptable to them and what would not.

I fall into the nesting-is-acceptable camp, but I can articulate when to nest. When the relationship is **one-to-many**, nest away. If the relationship is **one-to-one** or **many-to-one** (each book review can belong to only one reviewer), it should probably just be a property of the parent. If the relationship is **many-to-many** (authors may write multiple books, books may have more than one author), then both resources belong at the top level: `/books/REST-Assured` and `/authors/Tuttle-Adam-42`. In this case, if you wanted to find all books by an author, you would specify it as a filter parameter: `/books?author=Tuttle-Adam-42`.

Rate Limiting

If you choose to rate-limit your API, there are a few things you can do to make the experience easier for consumers. Use the status code **429 Too Many Requests** once their quota has been exceeded, but don't blind side them! Include the following headers with all requests to indicate current rate limiting status:

```
X-Rate-Limit-Limit: (# Allowed Req / period)
X-Rate-Limit-Remaining: (# remaining / period)
X-Rate-Limit-Reset: (# seconds until period reset)
```

The numbers listed here are in an extremely usable format. If you provided the number of requests sent in the period, the client would have to use it to find out how many are remaining to decide whether to throttle back or pause — why not just tell them how many are remaining? And if you provide a timestamp instead of the number of seconds, not only must the client do a date and time comparison to figure out how much time is left in the period, they are also vulnerable to clock skew[22]. By providing the number of seconds remaining in the rate limiting period, you save them from the additional steps of math, and completely sidestep clock skew.

Avoid Data Envelopes

Especially in enterprise environments where many developers are coming from a SOAP or XML-RPC background, data envelopes are very common. A data envelope is the practice of wrapping the requested data in a set of metadata that indicates whether or not there was an error, includes error messages if there were any, possibly more metadata, and finally includes the requested data:

```
{
  "success": false
  "errors": [
    "First Name is required",
    "Email is required"
  ]
  "data": null
}
```

The problem here is that you are reinventing the wheel. The `success` attribute duplicates the job of the status code, and needs the `errors` attribute to match the additional context it provides. Ninety-nine times out of one hundred, reinventing the wheel is a bad idea. If you are going to do it, do so with your eyes open.

---

[22]http://en.wikipedia.org/wiki/Clock_skew

Here's a use case where a Response Envelope could be a good thing: JSONP does not allow the client to see the response headers. Anything important, including success indication, needs to be in the response body. In this case, my recommendation is to support an ?envelope=true option for JSONP clients to specially request.

Consistent Error Payloads

If you are not using a standard response envelope (and to reiterate, you probably should not), then you should decide what your errors will look like, and be consistent with them across all resources. Usually a simple errors array of message strings is good enough to get the job done. In more sophisticated services, you may want to include more, like perhaps a stack trace. What you include is entirely up to you, just be consistent. And if error formatting needs to change and it breaks backwards compatibility, this too should cause a version number increase.

For what it's worth, there is an RFC[23] for error response payloads in JSON APIs. It defines properties: type, title, detail and instance and allows for additional attributes as necessary to make your response useful. It graduated from a draft to an RFC in 2016, but has not gained widespread adoption yet.

Searchable Collections

An API that houses large amounts of data without the ability to search can be a nightmare to work with. Basic searching is a relatively easy thing to accomplish. You designate a query parameter for searching, and then use it to filter the collection somehow:

```
GET /books?q=Tuttle
```

Note that I have searched for a value that will likely be listed as a property available only through a relationship (author name). How you setup your search is up to you, but the most important thing to think about is how users and developers will want to use your

---

[23] https://datatracker.ietf.org/doc/rfc7807/?include_text=1

search. In some cases it may make sense to make related resources searchable.

Alternatively to basic search, or perhaps in conjunction with it, you can also provide direct filtering. If our books collection also has tags and a title attribute, we can allow explicit filtering of these properties as well:

```
GET /books?title=REST&tags=Programming
```

The details of how you implement filtering are up to you, too. Do you need to support multiple tags? Wildcard searching in text fields? The sky is the limit.

Anti-Patterns (Red Flags)

Status: 200 Error: 200 means success, not Error. You're driving backwards down a busy freeway. It's only a matter of time until you crash.

GET Modifies Data: GET is supposed to be safe for web-spidering robots to follow and repeat as necessary. If you change data based on a GET, you are endangering your data. Is there a Data Protective Services we can call to report you?

A Sequence of requests is required to complete a task: REST is stateless. Everything needed to complete a request should be included in that single request. Splitting a task between multiple requests makes your API fragile and your data untrustworthy.

Use of Cookies or Sessions: Sessions usually require cookies, so these are kind of the same thing. Authentication is often required for APIs, but that is not the same thing as a logged-in session. The server is supposed to be allowed to forget that you made a request 30 seconds ago, if it wants to.

No ability to request an individual record: This is just crappy API design and lack of forethought. I have worked with too many crappy APIs to write a whole book on REST without specifically saying this: Allow individual record selection. And a decent search, too.

HATEOAS?

There is, of course, one more best practice that no doubt many of you were expecting in this chapter: HATEOAS. But isn't this chapter already long enough as it is? And if you were expecting its inclusion, then you know it is not a quick and simple topic to cover. No, HATEOAS gets its own chapter.

5: HATEOAS

Hypermedia As The Engine Of Application State is the idea that the root URL of the API is all that you must know in advance of using the API, and that all other resources and their available methods and properties should be discoverable from the responses you get back from the API. Each response from the API should provide links to related resources that the client can follow to get additional information. And in so doing, you should be able to forego out-of-band documentation about your API.

Proponents of HATEOAS say that after the entry point the actual URI should not matter; that it could just as easily be a random string of letters and numbers, and that the client should be able to follow the links from the entry point. Sounds great in concept, right? There's a certain amount of truth and appeal to the idea. If it isn't clear yet, I am not a HATEOAS fan.

When you start to implement it, you very quickly find yourself asking questions for which answers are not readily available. For starters, what should this entry point resource look like? It doesn't seem very RESTful to me to have a resource dedicated to listing your other resources, but let's give it the benefit of the doubt and list them anyway. Let's call this index of resources `/v1/index`.

To keep line-length down in the sample code I'm only going to include the URI, but in practice you should use the fully qualified URL, beginning with `http(s)://....`

```
{
    "resources": [
        {
            "rel": "books"
            ,"url": "/v1/books"
        }
        ,{
```

```
                "rel": "authors"
                ,"url": "/v1/authors"
            }
            ,{
                "rel": "reviews"
                ,"url": "/v1/reviews"
            }
        ]
    }
```

Assuming for the time being that this index of sorts is an acceptable place to start for HATEOAS —and assume we must, because there are no canonical reference APIs or documentation on what the entry point should look like or even be named— this only raises more questions. Should each resource in the list also include a list of allowed methods? Perhaps not, since we can get that from an `OPTIONS` request. What about available properties, and optional parameters like pagination, searching, filtering, and sorting? Those aren't usually available in `OPTIONS` responses. If we continue adding information to the index, at some point it begins to resemble a SOAP WSDL document; which is for many people a primary motivator for using *anything other than SOAP*. Despite the S in SOAP standing for Simple, it is not, and WSDL has a lot to do with that.

For now let's assume that what we've already described in the index is enough, and the client should follow the links to find out more information. It may request `GET /v1/books`, and get back a response not unlike this one:

```
    Link: <http://.../v1/books?page=2>; rel="next",
        <http://.../v1/books?page=434>; rel="last",
        <http://.../v1/books?page=1>; rel="first"
    [
        {
            "uri": "/v1/books/REST-Assured-5483902"
            ,"title": "REST Assured"
```

```
        ,"author": "/v1/authors/Tuttle-
Adam-4289047"
        ,"published": "2014-12-19 12:00:00 PM"
        ,"category": "Non-Fiction"
        ,"tags":
    [ "Internet","Programming","API","Reference" ]
    }
]
```

But even that relies upon an assumption that the GET method is supported for `/v1/books`. Instead, the HATEOAS fans would probably have you first request `OPTIONS /v1/books`, similar to pre-flighting a CORS AJAX request, to get the list of allowed methods. Either that or make your `GET` request but be prepared to get a **405 Method Not Allowed** response, on the off chance that you guessed wrong.

What if we want to update or delete a book? How do we know if this is allowed? Without out-of-band documentation we must start by making an `OPTIONS` request for the URI provided in the collection we previously requested:

```
OPTIONS /v1/books/REST-Assured-5483902
```

If the response header `Access-Control-Allow-Methods` contains `DELETE`, then we're allowed to delete this book:

```
DELETE /v1/books/REST-Assured-5483902
```

Unfortunately, this means yet again making two requests where one should suffice. Additionally, it may require pre-flighting every record in a result set in order to establish what controls to display to an end-user. You wouldn't display a delete button and wait for it to be clicked to pre-flight the `DELETE` request, and then reject the delete action if disallowed. The better user experience —not showing the delete button to begin with— requires knowing more information up front.

If you primarily create REST APIs to interact with mobile browsers, you find yourself embroiled in a battle between REST best practices (assuming you buy into HATEOAS), and mobile best practices, which teach you to minimize the number of network requests. Granted, `OPTIONS` requests are lightweight, but if you preflight every `GET` request, you may come close to doubling the number of network requests the client must make. It doesn't matter how fast those additional requests are: N+1 will take longer than N on its own because of the overhead involved in sending and receiving the request, as well as any network latency. Obviously one request will be faster than two. Since you can't satisfy both restraints, you must choose between earning Fielding's praise for your adherence to his ideals, or making your API faster.

From the `Link` header included with the response to our `GET /v1/books` request (which we pre-approved with an `OPTIONS /v1/books` request), we know that there are multiple pages to this collection, and we can easily jump to the first, last, next (and when applicable, previous) pages by following the provided links. The `Link` header is becoming a convention by virtue of its popularity; but what about other actions? What if your API supports searching or filtering books, and custom-sorting? How do you, as the API designer, communicate this to the client? No standard headers exist to indicate these intents.

You could make one up, but it will still require "training" the client. If you just made it up, there's no chance the client will understand what your new header is for when it arrives. You might be able to wedge them into the `Link` header with a `rel="search"`, but how exactly do you indicate where to inject the search string, and what values are valid to search with? Imagine if the `Link` header included:

```
</v1/books?q=:search&sort=:sort>; rel="search"
```

This is fairly intuitively understood by a human looking at it, but a program won't know what to do with it until a human tells it how to use these links. And `:search` could just as easily be `{search}`, or `$search` or many other possibilities. Somewhere along the line, someone has to tell the client how to use these special links.

The point is: at some point you have to have *some* documentation about *some* aspects of your API. Why try to eschew documentation completely, when it is practically impossible given an API of any reasonable complexity? And if you *have to* write some documentation, why jump through all of these hoops to put links to everything in the responses?

Practically speaking, unless they have been pre-warned, your average API consuming developer is going to expect that URIs will not change, at least in the current version, and will hard-code them into their client. But what if you did warn your consumers that URIs may change at any time? Would you expect them to start every request by requesting the index and following links all the way to the desired document again? That seems completely unreasonable to me.

HATEOAS is Fine for Websites

You know where HATEOAS works well? Websites. The data returned in responses —documents of HTML— have well defined expressive modes for linking to other bits of data and explaining what actions are available.

To me, HATEOAS smells like an unfinished attempt to refactor a pattern out of the way that websites work into something useful for API's. I say skip it and get back to work writing your application logic.

Is WADL The Answer?

Web Application Description Language, or WADL (pronounced "waddle") for short, is essentially a port of WSDL to REST. It is an XML document that is supposed to describe the resources in an API and their relationships; and although it was submitted to the W3C in 2009, they currently have no plans to standardize it.[24]

To add insult to injury, it has not seen widespread adoption thus far, so anyone pushing to use it is fighting an uphill battle. On the face of it, WADL seems like it might not be an altogether terrible idea for solving some of the problems I described with HATEOAS above. If

---

[24]http://www.w3.org/Submission/2009/03/Comment

you can automate the generation of your WADL documents, you might be inclined to pursue that. Anyone without WADL generation tooling will probably skip it, as creating and maintaining a complex XML document defining every aspect of their API could be just as much work as, if not more than, maintaining the API — and simply having a manually-created WADL adds brittleness to your API that HATEOAS is intended to eliminate. WADL's complexity and verbosity are antithetical to the lean and simple attitude that informs everything else about REST.

All of this is to say that I fundamentally disagree with the apparent goals and resulting mechanisms of HATEOAS (and WADL, too). Magically automated integration between disparate systems without need for documentation is at best something that requires a high level of complexity to accomplish (and thus not a good fit for the lean simplicity of REST), and is at worst a pipe dream.

6: Concrete Examples with Taffy

As I mentioned in the introduction, I created Taffy, the most popular framework for developing REST APIs on CFML platforms like ColdFusion and Lucee. It is only natural, then, that I should provide examples of all of these topics in the syntax that I helped design.

For the uninitiated, CFML was one of the pioneering languages for connecting web pages to databases, and it remains in active development today with major releases every two to three years. In addition to the commercial ColdFusion platform provided by Adobe[25], there is a free and open source alternative platform named Lucee[26], which aims to provide feature parity with ColdFusion where possible.

If CFML is new to you, I think you'll find that it mostly resembles JavaScript, with some extra bits here and there that should be mostly intuitive.

As this is not a book about Taffy, I will only be showing enough code to explain the concepts. Full documentation for Taffy is available at docs.taffy.io.

---

[25] http://adobe.com/go/coldfusion

[26] https://lucee.org/

Application.cfc and index.cfm

The core of every CFML application is an `Application.cfc` file and REST APIs are no different.

```
component extends="taffy.core.api" {
    this.name = "my_api";
    variables.framework = {
        //tweaks to the default config go here
    };
}
```

The key attribute is `extends="taffy.core.api"`. This imports most of the code that makes Taffy work: the routing engine and a few other bits and pieces.

In addition, as a front-controller framework, Taffy needs a central file for all requests to funnel through to allow its routing engine to work. The standard in CFML applications is to use `index.cfm`. In Taffy APIs, your `index.cfm` file can be blank (or not — but its code won't actually be executed), but it must exist.

At this point you have a functioning API with no resources defined. Every request will result in a 404; but it will be a RESTful 404.

Basic Resources

The next thing your API needs is resources. Let's start with a simple hello world example:

resources/hello.cfc:

```
component extends="taffy.core.resource"
taffy:uri="/hello" {
    function get(){
        return rep({message:"Hello, world!"}).withStatus(200, "OK");
    }
}
```

This class imports functionality from the base class `taffy.core.resource`, and registers the URI `/hello` with the routing engine. By virtue of implementing a method named `get` (case-insensitive), the `GET` HTTP method is allowed. For this resource, `POST`, `PUT`, `DELETE`, etc requests will all return a 405. `OPTIONS` is available and handled automatically by Taffy.

The implemented `get` method just returns a hard-coded object with a simple message. `rep()` is a shorthand alias for `representationOf()`, which is designed to reinforce the fact that the resource is not returning JSON-serialized data, it is returning a native object, which Taffy will serialize to JSON —its default mime type— before responding to the request. We have also chained the `rep()` call with `.withStatus()` to set the response status code and status text. Of course, the default is `200 OK` and the `.withStatus()` call is unnecessary in this case, but this is where you can set a different value when you need it.

When a client requests `GET /index.cfm/hello` the server will respond thusly:

```
HTTP/1.1 200 OK
Content-Type: application/json

{"message":"Hello world!"}
```

Note that you have only written 10 lines of code thus far — and that is rounding up for closing braces and counting the empty configuration object. Taffy prioritizes terseness, clean syntax, and semantically correct URI's over anything else. It uses convention instead of configuration whenever possible, and attempts to use inline metadata (e.g. `taffy:uri="..."`) rather than a central configuration file, wherever possible.

Many people find it undesirable to have an `/index.cfm` prefix in their URIs, but this is easily removed with URL Rewriting. However, I will leave it in for the remainder of the examples for the sake of added clarity.

Additional Verbs

The resource we defined supports the GET method because it has a get() function within. If we add a delete() function, the DELETE verb will be supported. The same is true for POST, PUT, HEAD, and PATCH, too. Taffy also supports HTTP method tunneling through the use of the X-HTTP-Method-Override header.

URI Tokens

How would you implement a URI like /widgets/42 in Taffy so that the value 42 becomes available to the handler? URI Tokens: First we will change our URI to /widgets/{widgetId}. Taffy will recognize anything inside curly-braces as a token and will allow any value in its position, except a forward slash. Whatever you name your URI token, you will need to add an identically named argument to all handler methods in the class:

```
function get( required numeric widgetId ){ /* ...
*/ }
```

In this example, Taffy will recognize 42 as the token widgetId and pass it as the widgetId value to the appropriate handler method.

In Taffy, all URI tokens are required for all handler methods in a resource. If you want to use a slightly different URI, that should be considered a different resource, and as such it belongs in a separate CFC.

(De)Serialization

I mentioned previously that Taffy expects your resources to return native data and will automatically serialize it to JSON (by default) before returning it to the client. Similarly, Taffy is capable of handling both JSON and url-encoded (e.g. application/x-www-form-urlencoded) request bodies. After deserialization, all keys are passed by name, with any URI tokens and query string parameters, to the appropriate handler method.

Taffy also supports the use of custom serializer and/or deserializer classes that you may provide, which would respectively enable you to return and/or accept XML, YAML, or any other serialization format you prefer. Below is the code for the default serializer. Providing a custom serializer is as simple as writing a clone of this class that returns your preferred format instead of JSON:

```
component extends="taffy.core.baseSerializer" {
    function getAsJson() taffy:default="true"
    taffy:mime="application/json;text/json" {
        return serializeJSON( variables.data );
    }
}
```

In order to support both the mime-type method for specifying requested return format and the "file extension" (e.g. .json URI suffix) method, Taffy uses two parts of this code to register this method as the handler for both. First, the metadata in the taffy:mime attribute is used to map the function to the mime type(s) listed. Second, the function is named using the file extension. Your serializer may have as many getAsX() methods as you like, where X is a format that you want to support (JSON, YAML, etc). The X portion of the method name is registered as a supported "file name" suffix and mapped to the same handler method.

Likewise, below is a simplified version of the default deserializer class. You may optionally implement your own deserializer to support as many input data formats as you like.

```
component extends="taffy.core.baseDeserializer" {
    function getFromJson(body)
    taffy:mime="application/json,text/json"
    {
        var response = {};
        var data = deserializeJSON( arguments.body );
        if ( !isStruct( data ) ){
            response[ '_body' ] = data;
        } else {
```

```
            response = data;
        }
        return response;
    }
}
```

Query String Parameters

This one is simple. If your handler method accepts an optional parameter:

```
function get( numeric page ){ /* ... */ }
```

Then a query string parameter may be used to pass a value to it:

```
/widgets?page=8
```

The handler method defines its arguments, and the values it receives can come from URI tokens, from the request body, and from query string parameters. In the event of a naming collision, query string parameters are the lowest priority: a same-named property in the request body would take precedence. And same-named URI tokens take precedence over both body properties and query string parameters.

Versioning

There are two approaches to the URI-based versioning that I advocate for Taffy-powered API's. On one hand, you can simply copy your entire API folder, and the parent folder naming sets the version, as in: `/api/v1/index.cfm/widgets` based on the parent folder name and the metadata `taffy:uri="/widgets"`.

Alternatively, if you would like to keep everything in one application context, you may embed the version into the `taffy:uri` metadata, and create a new class with an updated version identifier in the URI metadata when you need to increase the version. In this case, the final URI will resemble: `/api/index.cfm/v1/widgets` without a version-named parent folder and the version identifier embedded in the metadata as: `taffy:uri="/v1/widgets"`.

Of course, if you would like to reduce the number of classes that must be maintained, you may also embed the version as a URI token, as in: `taffy:uri="/{version}/widgets"`. In this case, all requests for widgets would go through the same class; but your logic would need to account for all possible api versions and could get very complex.

For the simplicity and ease of creating a new version by simply copying and renaming a single folder, I favor the first approach.

Inspecting Requests with onTaffyRequest

Taffy provides an event that you may listen for that executes for every request after the request has been parsed but before executing the requested resource. This event handler is named `onTaffyRequest()` and lives in your `Application.cfc` alongside `onApplicationStart()` and `onRequestStart()`. To it, Taffy passes a list of useful information:

- **verb** (string) - The HTTP request verb provided by the client

- **cfc** (string) - The CFC name (minus ".cfc") that would handle the request.

- **reqArgs** (struct) - A structure containing all of the arguments of the request, including tokens from the URI as well as any query string parameters, and the contents of the request body, if any.

- **ext** (string) - The mime extension (e.g. "json" - NOT the full mime type, e.g. "application/json")

- **hdrs** (struct) - A structure containing each header from the request, as sent by the client.

- **meta** (struct) - A structure containing any non-taffy metadata set on the requested resource method.

- **uriMatch** (string) - The `taffy:uri` value, including un-replaced tokens, from the CFC that matches the request. (e.g. `/foo/{bar}`)

To allow the request to continue as planned, return `true`. If you wish to block the request for some reason, you must provide a valid REST response. You do this using the same syntax you would inside one of your Taffy resources:

```
return rep( /* some data */ ).withStatus(200);
```

Just as with resources, returning an empty response body is as easy as:

```
return noData().withStatus( 401 ).withHeaders( {"X-Foo":"bar"} );
```

HTTP Basic Authentication

Taffy provides some helper methods for getting HTTP Basic Authentication data when the client sends it. You may call `getBasicAuthCredentials()` from within your `onTaffyRequest()`, and a structure with `username` and `password` keys will be returned. If no basic auth information is included in the request, then the values for both keys will be empty strings.

Of course, if the username and password do not validate, you do not want to allow the request to continue. In this case, the most appropriate course of action is to return from `onTaffyRequest()` as follows:

```
function onTaffyRequest( verb, cfc, reqArgs, ext, hdrs, meta, uriMatch ){
    if (/* fails auth credential check */){
        var body = {msg:"Bad password"};
        var headers = {"WWW-Authenticate": 'Basic realm="widgets"'};
        return rep( body ).withStatus( 401 ).withHeaders( headers );
    }
```

}

Inline Key Provisioning

As previously mentioned, I like to consider this approach a form of key creation, and as such I do it as a POST to /apikeys:

```
component extends="taffy.core.resource"
taffy:uri="/apikeys" {

  function post(required username, required password){
    password = bcrypt(password);
    var authenticated = queryExecute("
      select userId
      from users
      where username = :u
      and password = :p
    ", {
      u: username
      ,p: password
    });
    if (authenticated.recordCount > 0){
      var newkey = createUUID();
      queryExecute("
        insert into apikeys (userid, apikey, createDateTime)
        values( :u, :k, current_timestamp )
      ",{
        u: authenticated.userId
        ,k: newkey
      });
      return rep({ apikey: newkey }).withStatus(201, "Key Created");
    }
  }
}
```

By the way, bcrypt is not a function made available to you by Taffy. Instead, it is left as an exercise[27] for the reader. This is a relatively simple model of how to do inline authentication and token provisioning. Once tokens have been provisioned, you should check their validity in `onTaffyRequest()`:

```
function
onTaffyRequest(verb,cfc,reqArgs,ext,hdrs,meta,uriMa
tch){
    if (!structKeyExists(reqArgs, "apikey")){
        return noData().withStatus(401);
    }
    var validated = queryExecute("
        select *
        from apikeys
        where key = :k
    ", {
        k: reqArgs.apikey
    });
    if (validated.recordCount > 0){
        return true;
    }else{
        return noData().withStatus(401);
    }
}
```

Cross Origin Resource Sharing (CORS)

You can enable CORS in Taffy by setting the following configuration value in `Application.cfc`:

```
variables.framework.allowCrossDomain = true;
```

---

[27] https://tutt.xyz/bcrypt

Setting it to true enables CORS for any website, which is not very secure. Alternatively, you can set it to a list of domains. This would allow CORS requests only from example.com and google.com:

```
variables.framework.allowCrossDomain = "https://
example.com; https://google.com";
```

JSONP

By default, Taffy disables jsonp. To enable it, set the following configuration value in Application.cfc:

```
variables.framework.jsonp = "callback";
```

This enables the client to specify their jsonp handler in your `callback` property, as in:

```
/api/v1/widgets?callback=jsonpHandler
```

Resulting in a response body along the lines of:

```
jsonpHandler([ /* ... */ ]);
```

It is more common to name the property "jsonp", so that the request will resemble:

```
/api/v1/widgets?jsonp=jsonpHandler
```

Rate Limiting

There are as many ways to skin this cat as there are stars in the night sky. You could use Redis or memcached, for example. But to keep things simple I developed an example that uses CFML's Query datatype and Query of Queries feature. Unfortunately, it is a bit long to include here. I've never been a fan of examples that span 3 or more pages. Instead, please refer to the fully working example code, in the github repository[28].

Caching Hooks

Taffy has 3 caching events that you can implement to enable custom response caching for GET requests:

---

[28] https://tutt.xyz/taffy-rate-limit

1. `setCachedResponse(cacheKey, data)`

2. `getCachedResponse(cacheKey)`

3. and `validCacheExists(cacheKey)`

The details are up to you to implement, so that you can use any caching mechanism you like. Some ideas include EhCache, Memcached, and Redis. The workflow is as follows:

1. During a successful `GET` request, after your resource returns data, Taffy will call `setCachedResponse` with a unique `cacheKey` string which identifies the URI & request arguments, and the data. Your implementation caches the value for the key.

2. In a subsequent identical `GET` request, Taffy will call `validCacheExists` with the same `cacheKey` string. If your cache has a value for this cacheKey, and it is not expired or otherwise invalid, return true — else return false.

3. If your `validCacheExists` function returned true, Taffy will call `getCachedResponse` with the same `cacheKey` string, *instead of executing the resource method.* Your implementation of `getCachedResponse` should return the cached value, which will then be serialized and sent back to the client.

ETags

Taffy's implementation of ETags is completely transparent to the developer. Simply set `variables.framework.useEtags = true;` in your `Application.cfc` configuration, and the ETag headers will be generated and sent with responses automatically, and `If-None-Match` headers will automatically be handled accordingly. `If-Match` is not yet supported.

Error Handling

Taffy has an interesting mechanism for logging errors that bubble up to the global level. You are free to try/catch and suppress errors as you see fit, of course; but anything that bubbles up to the global level is handled with a global error handler.

By default, Taffy does nothing to log your error messages. (An earlier version was configured to send error emails, but used a dummy email address, resulting in *quite a lot* of undeliverable email sitting in people's mail spools.) But this does not mean that the error information is not displayed. Instead of logging, the default behavior is to show information about the exception as a JSON object, with the exception summary and detailed message, as well as the stack trace available in the response body; and a status code of 500 is used.

Taffy comes bundled with some Logging Adapters that make it easy to send exception information to BugLogHQ[29], or Hoth[30], or to simply send yourself an email with the exception information. To enable an exception log adapter, configure it[31] as follows:

```
variables.framework = {
    exceptionLogAdapter: "taffy.bonus.LogToBugLogHQ"
    ,exceptionLogAdapterConfig: {
        bugLogListener = "bugLog.listeners.bugLogListenerWS"
        ,bugEmailRecipients = "you@yourdomain.com"
        ,bugEmailSender = "errors@yourdomain.com"
        ,hostname = cgi.host_name
        ,apikey = "your-bugloghq-api-key"
    }
};
```

---

[29] http://bugloghq.com/

[30] https://github.com/aarongreenlee/Hoth

[31] https://github.com/atuttle/Taffy/wiki/Exception-Logging-Adapters

This configuration specifies that exceptions should be sent to my local instance of BugLogHQ for logging; that if BugLogHQ is unreachable for some reason, an email should be sent from errors@yourdomain.com to you@yourdomain.com. The apikey is what allows the request (if your BugLogHQ instance requires one), and the hostname identifies the server in the bug logs.

Conclusion

I hope I have convinced you that REST APIs are worth your time and effort, but that trying to identify every letter of the law, and stick to it, is not necessarily a worthwhile goal to pursue. Remember: Getting work done should take priority over pie in the sky ideals about what makes something "RESTful" according to academics or internet commenters.

Don't reinvent the wheel. Remember your verbs and status codes. Use sane URIs. Version your API before it ever sees daylight. Be consistent. Do these things and you are already 90% of the way there.

> *" I'd far rather be happy than right any day. "*
> —Douglas Adams, **The Hitchhiker's Guide to the Galaxy**

Thank You

I owe a tremendous debt of gratitude to many people, most of all my wife Megan; in part for allowing me to cut corners on some of my family responsibilities while writing, but most of all for her moral support and believing in me despite having no idea what this book is about or why anyone would want to read it. True love!

It was the tireless efforts of Daniel Short that shielded you from what I can only assume are the spelling and grammar mistakes that sneak in when burning the candle at both ends. Without the encouragement and interest of the people on the Taffy Users mailing list, there would be no book.

Finally, thank you dear reader, for believing in a self-publishing author enough to spend some of your hard-earned cash in exchange for the promise of knowledge exchange. Thanks for taking a chance.

Appendix 1: Common HTTP Statuses

200 OK What it says on the tin.

201 Created Insert successful.

202 Accepted Insert accepted but queued.

204 No Content Like a 200, but empty body.

301 Moved Permanently Moved, update your links.

302 Found Moved temporarily, just redirect, don't update links.

304 Not Modified Your local cache is still good, don't update.

400 Bad Request General purpose catch-all for client errors.

401 Unauthorized "I don't know who you are."

402 Payment Required "Nice try. Pay first."

403 Forbidden "I know you. You're not allowed to do that."

404 Not Found Not found.

405 Method Not Allowed Found; verb not supported on URI.

406 Not Acceptable Can't return req resource in req format.

409 Conflict Refusal to update due to a conflict.

410 Gone Req resource *used to* be available, but is now gone.

420 Enhance Your Calm Rate limit almost exceeded.

429 Too Many Requests Rate limit exceeded.

500 Server Error General purpose catch-all for server errors.

501 Not Implemented Server doesn't recognize the req method.

503 Service Unavailable App server unreachable or timed out.

509 Bandwidth Limit Exceeded For quota enforcement.

Appendix 2: Some History, If You Want It

When people argue about REST on Hacker News today, they point to Roy Fielding's 2000 Dissertation[32] as the defining document. You might be shocked to learn that Fielding did not invent REST — at least not the techniques described. His dissertation served to codify behaviors already in practice, in most cases, and to bless a specific set of them as what he coined REST. Unfortunately, it reads like an academic dissertation and not a technical manual. There are what appear to be ambiguities and incomplete concepts, to the layman such as myself. It is impossible to read and comprehend without several re-readings and copious annotating; and even then his intentions may remain unclear.

Think back to the mid 1990's. Bill Clinton was the President of the United States. JavaScript was just getting started. **Internet Explorer was innovative.** In 1996 the `<iframe>` tag was introduced for asynchronous content loading. In 1999 Microsoft used iframes to rotate content on the Internet Explorer default home page; and IE5 was released with the XMLHTTP ActiveX control, later adapted by other browsers into the XMLHttpRequest ("XHR") JavaScript object. Internet Explorer finally adopted the native JavaScript XHR object in IE7, though the ActiveX version remains supported through IE11. Microsoft's Edge browser does not support ActiveX. Asynchronous content loading remained a parlor trick until 2000 when Outlook Web App used it to load application data without the need for page reloads, delivering a superior user experience to anything else available at the time.

Remember, 2000 was also the year that Fielding published his dissertation, and coined the term REST.

---

[32] http://www.ics.uci.edu/~fielding/pubs/dissertation/rest_arch_style.htm

In 2004 Google released Gmail, the first massively adopted, standards-compliant, cross-browser AJAX application. They followed suit again in 2005 with Google Maps. The term AJAX wouldn't be coined until a February 2005 blog post by Jesse James Garrett.[33]

In April of 2006, the W3C — the standards body of the internet — released the very first draft spec for XMLHttpRequest to codify the burgeoning web standard.

In 2008, apparently offended by what people had been referring to as RESTful APIs, Fielding took to his blog to pen another academically impenetrable article listing six commandments of REST, including:

> *A REST API should be entered with no prior knowledge beyond the initial URI (bookmark) and set of standardized media types that are appropriate for the intended audience (i.e., expected to be understood by any client that might use the API). From that point on, all application state transitions must be driven by client selection of server-provided choices that are present in the received representations or implied by the user's manipulation of those representations. The transitions may be determined (or limited by) the client's knowledge of media types and resource communication mechanisms, both of which may be improved on-the-fly (e.g., code-on-demand). [Failure here implies that out-of-band information is driving interaction instead of hypertext.]*

What he's bemoaning here is a concept commonly referred to as HATEOAS, or Hypermedia As The Engine Of Application State — specifically the apparent inability of developers to implement it to his liking. It sounds good on paper when you're only writing *about* the concept, but when you start to implement it you find yourself asking questions to which Fielding has conveniently failed to provide an

---

[33] http://www.adaptivepath.com/ideas/ajax-new-approach-web-applications/

answer. I have obliged you with gobs of my own opinions on HATEOAS in chapter 5.

In 2008 Martin Fowler threw his weight behind HATEOAS, too[34]; but he too falls prey to exactly the same problem.

While Fielding deserves credit for coining the term REST and first recognizing the usefulness of a standard for its use, we are not bound to abide his every word on the matter. Every bite of armchair direction we swallow should be seasoned with a healthy pinch of pragmatism. Just as common use can redefine "literally" to mean "figuratively"[35] (!!), common use can redefine REST to mean whatever the community agrees upon (decided by commonality). As Hacker News commenter jayvanguard so eloquently put it:

> *This debate was settled almost a decade ago. URL forms don't matter in theoretical dissertation REST, but 15 years of practice has firmly decided they are indeed a core part of real-world REST.*
>
> *HTTP based web services existed before Roy's dissertation and while the formalizing of them helped them mature rapidly, the idealistic principles aren't the final word on the subject anymore. Real world practice now is.*

Based on commonality in my own experience, and the commonality of advice I've read over the last 10+ years, my best understanding of REST is as follows:

- REST is CRUD over HTTP. Some exceptions to this rule are allowed as long as they don't become the rule.

- Don't needlessly reinvent features that already exist in HTTP:

---

[34] http://martinfowler.com/articles/richardsonMaturityModel.html

[35] Note the "informal" definition: https://www.google.com/search?q=define+literally

- Status Codes

- URIs

- Verbs

- Headers

- Request/response body contains only **data**

- Basic Auth

I don't claim that this is a perfect and complete picture of the best possible implementation of REST. But it's the pragmatic place to start.

History influences practice, but common practice can redefine history, too.

Appendix 3: Close to the Metal

If we're going to discuss CRUD over HTTP in detail, I should at least offer to show you what HTTP requests and responses look like. This information is not strictly necessary for a healthy understanding of REST principles. But if you're intellectually curious about how HTTP works, read on. Heck, even follow along with your favorite telnet client. Telnet, of course, allows you to make a raw HTTP request and view the response.

The first thing we'll do is open a connection to a server at Google, on port 80 (HTTP):

```
$ telnet www.google.com 80
Trying 65.199.32.57...
Connected to www.google.com.
Escape character is '^]'.
```

We're now connected. Let's send a request for the google homepage, specifying that we will use HTTP 1.1 syntax. We must also include the `Host` header to indicate which website we're accessing, because each server may be responsible for more than one website, and each may have its own index.html. Here we're specifying the `GET` verb. The URI is `/index.html`.

```
GET /index.html HTTP/1.1
Host: www.google.com
```

Like the Python programming language, whitespace matters. Lines must not be indented, and after the two lines above we must send a blank line to indicate the request is complete. Likewise, this indicates that we may not include any blank lines in the middle of our request, because they will cause everything after the blank line to be ignored.

Having processed our request and found what we asked for, it responds:

```
HTTP/1.1 200 OK
```

```
Date: Mon, 01 Dec 2014 03:18:09 GMT

Expires: -1

Cache-Control: private, max-age=0

Content-Type: text/html; charset=ISO-8859-1

Set-Cookie: <snip>

Server: gws

X-XSS-Protection: 1; mode=block

X-Frame-Options: SAMEORIGIN

Alternate-Protocol: 80:quic,p=0.002

Transfer-Encoding: chunked


<!doctype html>...
```

Here we can see that the server has responded using the HTTP/1.1 syntax, with status code 200 OK. The date and time of the response are given, along with a series of additional response headers. I have omitted the cookie contents to save space, and because they are irrelevant (even moreso when discussing APIs). The list of headers is considered complete once we reach the first blank line, and what follows is the response body; in this case an HTML page. After the response body is another blank line, and the connection is terminated by the server.

More or less this same sequence of events plays out for every page you request on the internet, as well as every external asset it includes: JavaScript and CSS files, images, videos, zip files, pdfs, and so forth.

REST APIs work exactly the same. The only major difference is that we're requesting and updating data, not web pages. When you post a new tweet from your phone, an HTTP request is made, POSTing some authentication headers and the content of your tweet as data to a URI that Twitter specifies. If your tweet succeeds, you get back a 200-series status code, indicating success, and your tweet is shared to your followers.

I am *literally* making this up (the actual Twitter API is pretty complex), but here's a sample of what a simple Tweet API might look like, without the authentication bits:

```
POST /tweets HTTP/1.1
Host: api.twitter.com
Accept: application/json
Content-Type: application/json
{"user":"@AdamTuttle","tweet":"I'm reading an awesome book right now."}
```

```
HTTP/1.1 201 Tweet Created
Date: Mon, 01 Dec 2014 03:19:00 GMT

{"id":436297432}
```

Let's say I want to delete the tweet that I just created. Since the previous API request returned my Tweet id, we can send a `DELETE` request to our fictitious api:

```
DELETE /tweets/436297432 HTTP/1.1
Host: api.twitter.com
```

```
HTTP/1.1 200 Tweet Deleted
Date: Mon, 01 Dec 2014 03:19:42 GMT
```

As you can see, API requests are just normal HTTP requests, with the added benefit that we get to make use of a wide range of HTTP verbs that do not see common use in normal web browsing. While it may seem like a superset of HTTP at first, it is actually just a more complete usage of what HTTP offers than what we are used to seeing in web applications.

www.ingramcontent.com/pod-product-compliance
Lightning Source LLC
Chambersburg PA
CBHW070441220526
45466CB00004B/1748